Mad about Cats

Kitty Bunton

summersdale

MAD ABOUT CATS

Copyright © Summersdale Publishers Ltd, 2006

Illustrations by Salma Conway

Summersdale Publishers Ltd
46 West Street
Chichester
West Sussex
PO19 1RP
UK

www.summersdale.com

ISBN: 1-84024-518-2

ISBN: 978-1-84024-518-9

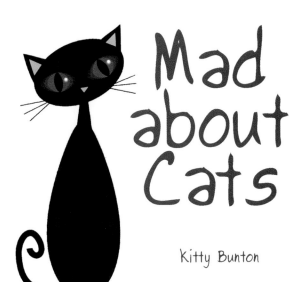

Mad about Cats

Kitty Bunton

You know you're mad about cats when...

You keep a snippet of your cat's fur in a locket.

You agonise more over getting your cat neutered than you do about giving your kids the MMR jab.

Your will states that upon death, your entire estate goes to your cat... partly because no one else wants to inherit several rusty tins of Whiskas.

You've converted your spare room into a battery fish farm.

Most kids have an imaginary friend. You had an imaginary cat.

You change your birth date and gain Chinese citizenship – just so you can tell people that you were born in the Year of the Cat.

You feed your cat GM foods in the hope that he'll grow big enough to kill the dog next door.

You know you're mad about cats when...

You develop RSI from
too much obsessive
cat stroking.

You put your newborn
baby up for adoption
because it wasn't
furry enough.

Dr Albert Schweitzer, the 1952 Nobel Peace Prize Winner, became ambidextrous in order to accommodate his cat Sizi. Whenever Sizi fell asleep on the doctor's arm, he would obediently write prescriptions with his other hand to avoid waking her.

Renowned scientist and philosopher Sir Isaac Newton was an ardent cat lover, who believed in preserving the liberty and dignity of the feline race. Thus, in order that his cats might wander in and out of his house at will as he continued his research uninterrupted, he created the very first cat-flap.

You want your cat to travel in style so you buy him a *Fur*rari.

You try to persuade your local police force to replace their dogs with cats, telling them it will improve paw and order.

You know you're mad about cats when...

Your freezer is full
of dead pigeons.

You refuse to admit
that your precious
tom is fat; he's just
horizontally challenged.

Your choice of holiday
depends on which
airport has the finest
cattery en route.

You know you're mad about cats when...

You hate dogs.

It was said that the famous poet Petrach loved his cat even more than his idolised lover, Laura. When he died, his adored pet was put down and mummified in remembrance of him.

Cardinal Richelieu, an influential French Cardinal of the sixteenth century, had a cattery constructed at Versailles especially for his cats, and employed a team of overseers to feed them chicken paté twice daily. Both the overseers and the cats were generously provided for in the Cardinal's will.

People never seem
relaxed in your living
room... perhaps
because it's full of glass-
encased stuffed cats
that you've loved and
lost over the years.

You know you're mad about cats when...

Instead of asking how your weekend was, your work colleagues ask how your cats are doing.

You know you're mad about cats when...

You've replaced photos
of your family with
stills from *Born Free.*

In order to share a
greater affinity with
your tom, you have a
'human-flap' installed.

You know you're mad about cats when...

You are investigated by
the RSPCA for keeping
mice especially for
your cat to hunt.

You know you're mad about cats when...

You own enough furry
felines to stage your
own production of *Cats.*

You eat from a bowl
on the kitchen floor
while your cat dines in
splendour at the table.

You get thrown out of your clay-modelling class when you attempt to sculpt a life-size Sphinx in the studio.

The prophet Mohammed's love of cats extended to ensuring the utmost comfort of his moggy Muezza. It is said that one day when he was being called to prayer he cut off the sleeve of his robe rather than disturb the sleeping cat.

An Egyptian sultan in the thirteenth century left his entire fortune to the stray cats of Cairo, his legacy ensuring that for years to come homeless and impoverished cats were entitled to receive a free daily meal.

You know you're mad about cats when...

You cry whenever
Jerry gets the upper
hand over Tom.

You insist your cat's
'*never* done that before'
when he jumps up on
the dinner table to steal
your guests' food.

The first two items on
your wedding list are a
fine crystal water bowl
and bone china dish so
kitty can dine in style.

You know you're mad about cats when...

You're late for work because you had to blow-dry and style kitty's fur.

You spend hours in the supermarket agonising over cat food: Tender Terrine with Rabbit and Chicken or Delicious Turkey Morsels in a Succulent Jelly?

You put your back out sleeping on a thin strip of the bed. Well, you wouldn't want to wake kitty, would you?

You are on first name terms with all the local firemen.

You teach your cat to read and write so that, on the very rare occasions when you're apart, you can still keep in touch.

Freddie Mercury owned a harem of cats – named Tom, Jerry, Oscar, Tiffany, Lily, Goliath, Miko, Romeo and Delilah. He loved them so dearly that he commissioned paintings of them all, and even wrote a song about his favourite, Delilah.

Inscription on the Royal Tombs at Thebes: 'Thou art the Great Cat, the avenger of the gods, and the judge of words, and the president of the sovereign chiefs and the governor of the holy Circle; thou art indeed... the Great Cat.'

You only ever date fellow cat-owners. The breaking point in your relationship comes when your respective cats meet for the first time...

Your refrigerator contains up to four different flavours of cat food at any time, each of which has been opened by you and rejected by your cat.

You have a Best Cat at your wedding. Naturally the speech is a tad disappointing but the imaginative way he wears his buttonhole keeps the guests amused.

You know you're mad about cats when...

You lose your job at the pet shop because you refuse to sell any of the cats.

You get your photos developed… and there's not a single shot of a human being.

You know you're mad about cats when...

You have a bumper sticker which reads: 'You can never have enough cats.'

You sit through mind-numbing adverts rather than risk disturbing the cat, who is sleeping peacefully on the remote.

Your choice of friends is determined by whether or not your cat likes them.

You know you're mad about cats when...

You never leave the
house... except to feed
stray cats in your street.

Your friend calls for
a chat and you won't
let them off the phone
until they've said a few
words to your cat.

You know you're mad about cats when...

Your cat sleeps on your head, and you like it.

You know you're mad about cats when...

You and your cat have
matching ID tags.

Friends no longer offer you the use of their lint brushes, having realised your battle with fur has long since been lost.

You know you're mad about cats when...

Your cat is introduced by
name to any newcomer
to your house.

You don't understand why people make such a fuss about cats leaving 'scratch marks'; they're merely personalising the upholstery.

Raymond Chandler regarded his black Persian, named Taki, as though she were human. Taki had developed the habit of sitting on his manuscripts as he tried to revise them, and so he often referred to her as his 'secretary'.

Mark Twain's daughter Susy once observed of her father, 'The difference between Papa and Mamma is that Mamma loves morals and Papa loves cats.' The highly esteemed writer had no fewer than eleven cats, who all lived with him on his farm in Connecticut.

You're a great cook.
As long as it's
Kitekat or Sheba.

The Paris home of Swiss artist
Theophile Steinlen was christened
'Cats Corner' due to his tendency
to incorporate his beloved cats
into most of his designs.

Jock, the favourite orange tabby of Sir Winston Churchill, slept in his master's bed every night and attended wartime cabinet meetings.

You and your friends
bunch up on a tiny sofa
while your cat stretches
out on his very own
luxury armchair.

You know you're mad about cats when...

You and your spouse got rid of the kids... because the cat was allergic.

You've taken to wearing a
necklace fitted with a bell.

Your neighbour suspects
you of dealing drugs but
when the police search
your property, all they
find is a greenhouse
full of catnip.

Eighteenth-century writer Samuel Johnson doted upon his pet cat, Hodge. This pampered moggy dined on oysters fetched by Johnson himself, who preferred not to entrust this important job to one of his servants.

Artist and author Edward Lear owned a pet tabby named Foss, who was the inspiration for the drawings which accompanied his famous rhyme, 'The Owl and the Pussycat'. When Lear decided to move to San Remo in Italy, he employed an architect to design and build an exact likeness of his English home, to minimise stress caused to Foss during the move.

You know you're mad about cats when...

You renounce your
religion in favour
of Ancient Egyptian
cat-worship.

You know you're mad about cats when...

You count kittens,
not sheep.

www.summersdale.com